Everything You Need to Know About

CONFLICT
RESOLUTION

Conflicts can happen anywhere and at any time.

• THE NEED TO KNOW LIBRARY •

Everything You Need to Know About

CONFLICT RESOLUTION

Amy Nathan

THE ROSEN PUBLISHING GROUP, INC.
NEW YORK

Acknowledgments
Thanks to the following people for describing their conflict resolution
programs and arranging for some of their students to fill out questionnaires or
be interviewed about their experiences: Angela Callahan, Robert Poole, Middle
School, Baltimore, Maryland; Bob Fatchett, Tappan Middle School, and Jim
Sweigart, Pioneer High School, Ann Arbor, Michigan; Sharon Watson, Project
Reach Youth, New York. Thanks also to Alan Borer, Director, Guidance
Support Services, New York City Board of Education.

Published in 1996 by The Rosen Publishing Group, Inc.
29 East 21st Street, New York, NY 10010

Copyright 1996 by The Rosen Publishing Group, Inc.

First Edition

Manufactured in the United States of America

Library of Congress Cataloging-in-Publication Data

Nathan, Amy.
    Everything you need to know about conflict resolution / Amy
Nathan.
        p.   cm. — (The need to know library)
    Includes bibliographical references and index.
    ISBN 0-8239-2058-5
    1. Peer counseling of students.   2. Conflict management—Study and
teaching.   3. Problem solving—Study and teaching.   I. Title.
II. Series.
LB1027.5.N249   1996
371.4′6—dc20   95-40195
                                                                              CIP
                                                                               AC

Contents

There are ways to solve a conflict without using physical force.

Introduction

*T*he trouble started quickly. One minute Tom was walking down the school hall. The next minute he was sprawled on the floor. A friend had tripped him.

That made Tom angry. He got up, glared at his friend, and gave him a push. The friend shoved Tom back. "There we were in the hall, pushing each other," said Tom.

What happened next? Did these teens throw some punches? Or did one stomp off, shouting a nasty comment at the other? Did they trade insults all day whenever they passed in the hall? Did one threaten to get even with the other after school? Did classmates spread rumors about the blowup between Tom and his friend? After school, did a crowd gather outside to watch the big fight?

Luckily, none of that happened.

Let's go back to the hallway where Tom was tripped. He suddenly stopped pushing and just stood there for a moment—thinking. Then he said, "Hey, let's not fight. I don't want to get suspended. Let's talk." So right there in the hall, Tom and his friend talked it out.

Conflict resolution teaches you to talk your problems out.

Each teen listened as the other told his side of the story. "My friend told me he tripped me because I had bumped into him," said Tom. "I didn't know I'd done that. I wasn't paying much attention as I walked down the hall. But my friend thought I bumped him on purpose. I said it was an accident. I said I was sorry. He apologized, too, for tripping me. We shook hands and were friends again." Case closed.

This is a true story. Why did Tom use words instead of fists to end that shoving match? Because he remembered what he had learned in a special course he had taken at school that taught him new ways to solve problems. Without the course, he probably would have reacted differently to being tripped. "That's the kind of thing I would have fought about in the past," he said. But he didn't, thanks to the skills he had learned—skills of conflict resolution.

In 1994, former U.S. president Jimmy Carter and Bosnian Serb leader Radovan Karadzic worked to resolve the conflict in Bosnia by negotiating a cease-fire agreement.

Chapter 1

What Is Conflict Resolution?

Conflicts happen all the time. They can range from a shoving match in school or a quarrel at home to disputes between huge companies or nations.

Conflict is part of life. You can't escape it. But you can learn to deal with it successfully. That's what conflict resolution is all about. Conflict resolution is a way of handling conflicts by talking problems out—not fighting them out. The goal is not just to end a conflict, but to *solve* the problem so that all sides feel satisfied. That's what "resolution" means: to deal with something successfully, to clear it up, to find an answer.

In conflict resolution, one side doesn't force its ideas on the other side. Instead, both sides talk and listen to each other. Both sides get a chance to explain how they see the situation. That lets each side come to understand the other's point of view. Then they negotiate—they discuss the problem and think up possible solutions. They keep on talking until they come up with a solution that both sides can support.

People who take training in conflict resolution learn how to do this kind of negotiating. You start by learning more about conflicts—why they happen, how people usually react to them. You learn how to think through a conflict so that you can figure out what it's really all about. You also learn special listening and talking skills that can help calm a conflict down so the people involved feel free to talk.

These basic skills of conflict resolution can then be put to use to solve a conflict in several ways:

The Do-It-Yourself Way. The two people involved in a conflict talk things out on their own. This can work even if only one of the two has been trained in conflict resolution. That was the case in Tom's tripping incident. Only Tom had taken a course in conflict resolution. But by using some of the skills he had learned, Tom helped his friend cool down so they could talk. Conflict resolution training suggests steps to follow in getting such a talk going.

The Get-Help-from-a-Mediator Way. Sometimes a conflict is so difficult that the people involved can't solve it on their own. Conflict resolution can still offer a way out. It's called mediation. A specially trained person called a

Couples who are having problems often use a mediator to help them.

mediator (or conflict manager) acts as referee for people in conflict. The mediator brings them together and helps them talk with each other until they reach an agreement. Mediators use the basic conflict resolution skills plus special ones.

Conflict Resolution Goes to School

Conflict resolution has been used for many years in the adult world. It has helped companies solve problems with workers. It has helped government officials make peace between countries. Judges have used the skills of conflict resolution to settle arguments among citizens.

Couples who are getting a divorce often have a mediator help them work out their differences.

In recent years, conflict resolution has also spread into the world of teens. In the 1960s and '70s, a few teachers began to introduce their students to this kind of nonviolent problem-solving. But it wasn't until the '80s and early '90s that conflict resolution really caught on in the schools.

The first school-based conflict resolution program was introduced in New York City schools in 1972. That was a time when fighting in school was on the rise. Millions of cases of assault, robbery, or theft on school property were reported each year. Schoolyard squabbles also were turning more deadly as some students employed guns or other weapons to settle a score. Newspaper headlines shouted about the violence in the schools. A study by the Centers for Disease Control several years ago found that one out of five high school students carried a gun, a knife, or a club to school. It has been estimated that about 16,000 thefts and violent crimes occur on or near school grounds on a daily basis. Teachers and principals also worry about the less violent kinds of disputes that often upset a school day, such as teasing, put-downs, and bullying. According to some reports, one in every ten kids is hassled regularly by a bully at school.

School officials realized that they had to help

Students can learn the skills of conflict resolution in their classes at school.

Some community centers teach conflict resolution skills.

students learn better ways to handle problems. Conflict resolution training seemed to offer a ray of hope. More and more schools began to teach this nonviolent method of solving conflicts. Today, more than 5,000 schools across the United States offer programs in conflict resolution. In some public schools, like those in Chicago, all students are required to take conflict resolution courses.

The School Programs

The programs are set up differently at different schools. In some schools, every student learns the skills of conflict resolution. They do this either in a special class or as part of a regular subject such as health, English, social studies, or even art.

Other schools involve students in conflict resolution through a peer mediation project. Students act as mediators when their peers (other students) have conflicts they can't solve on their own. Usually, only a few students are trained to be mediators.

Some schools offer both kinds of programs— conflict resolution classes for everyone as well as special training for peer mediators. Students in some schools have formed drama groups that spread the word by doing nonviolent problem-solving skits for other students. A few schools teach these problem-solving skills to teachers and parents as well as students. After all, it's hard to expect students to use the methods if the adults around them continue to bicker and squabble in the old-fashioned way. Some community centers also teach people—youngsters and adults—how to use the skills of conflict resolution.

As you may know from your own experience, learning is lively in conflict resolution classes. Students don't just sit and listen to lectures. They have to participate. They practice the new skills they're learning by doing skits or by role-playing. Instructors may set up pretend conflict situations and have students act them out, trying different ways to solve the conflict. Or students may work in small discussion groups to test their new skills. Students also get to explore their feelings about conflicts and discuss freely their ideas on many important issues.

This teaching style seems to appeal to students. "I really liked doing the role-playing," said one girl who took classes in conflict resolution. Another teen noted: "I got a better idea of what causes conflicts. I realized that many of them come from meaningless incidents that could have easily been talked out." A boy added that the training "makes you more aware of things that can happen in a conflict."

Chapter 2

A Look at Conflict

Before you can solve a conflict, you have to understand what it's about. The details of conflicts differ. But if you look closely, you'll see that many have a lot in common. Conflicts usually concern three basic kinds of issues:*

- **Conflicts over values.** These kinds of conflicts have to do with opinions that people hold very strongly. For example, the belief that cheating is wrong is a value many people have. If you hold this value, you will probably get into a conflict with a friend who wants you to pass him the answers for a test. A clash over which is the best rock band might also be considered a values conflict.

* Adapted from *Conflict Resolution: A Secondary School Curriculum* by Gail Sadalla, Manti Henriquez, Meg Holmberg (San Francisco: The Community Board Program, Inc., 1987).

Conflicts over things often arise when two people want the same item or object.

Values conflicts can be hard to solve. It's important to stick by your values, especially in situations that involve things that are illegal, dangerous, or just plain wrong. Often the best way out of a values conflict is for both sides to agree to disagree. They can talk with each other to learn each other's views; then they can simply accept the fact that they see things differently.

- **Conflicts over things.** An example of this kind of conflict would be two students fighting over a certain special pencil, or two kids bickering over the last slice of pizza. They want the same thing, but there's not enough for both.

- **Conflicts over psychological needs.** Respect, acceptance, control, independence, belonging, friendship—these are a few psychological needs. When people feel that these needs aren't being met or are being ignored, a conflict can develop.

   The boy who tripped Tom felt that Tom wasn't treating him with proper respect. Their conflict was about psychological needs. So are many of the conflicts that are started by gossip or rumors. "Most conflicts at our school start with rumors," a 17-year-old reported. "Little situations are blown way out of proportion and turn into big problems."

Digging Deeper

Many conflicts fit into more than one of those three groups. It can take a bit of digging (and talking) to figure that out. For example, Jenny and her friend bickered over a pencil. Was that just a simple "thing" conflict? Not exactly. Jenny was already ticked off with her friend before the pencil flare-up. How come? The friend hadn't returned Jenny's phone calls three nights in a row. So their conflict was about the pencil *and* about a psychological need—Jenny's need for acceptance and friendship. If they deal just with the pencil and not the feelings, they won't really solve the conflict.

A clash with your parent over a clothes allowance may also fit into more than one group. It

How you react in a conflict can affect the outcome of the situation.

may be about much more than money; it may be about a psychological need—your need for independence. The conflict may also concern values—your parent's belief in the importance of being thrifty and responsible. Solving this one will take more than a chat about cash.

How People React to Conflict

People often make conflicts worse by how they react. That includes people who throw punches as well as those who pull back. Conflict resolution programs help you think about what you usually do when you're in a conflict. That helps you see what changes you might want to make so that conflict-solving can come easier for you. Here are some common ways people react to conflict:

- **Blast it.** Some people see conflict as a win-lose situation. They feel that only they are right; the other side is wrong. They try to blast their way through a conflict so that they win and the other side loses. Some may do that by fighting. Others may overpower the other side with insults, put-downs, bribes, or threats.

  For example, Chuck and Greg are at the park and have only one basketball. Chuck wants to play a game of one-on-one. Greg wants to practice shooting three-pointers. Chuck tends to react to conflicts with confrontation. He blurts out, "It's my ball. You play my way or else you don't play." That threat could turn a small problem into a major battle. Even if Chuck gets his way without a fight, the conflict still won't have been completely solved. Greg will feel irritated. More conflicts are likely to bubble up between them later.

- **Avoid it.** Some people believe that conflict is bad and try to avoid it as much as possible. When a conflict comes up, they may ignore it. They may pretend it didn't really happen. Or they may always give in and smooth things over. That may make things better for a while. But in the long run, it may actually make them worse.

If solved well, conflicts can make relationships stronger.

If Greg goes along with Chuck's demand to
"play my way or else . . . ," he may avoid trouble
for now. But if he does that often, he'll get more
and more angry about always being put down.
That anger may build up until he explodes about
something else later.

- **Solve it.** Instead of ducking conflicts or blasting
their way out of them, some people try to face
conflicts fairly. They don't try to "win." Instead,
they look for the cause of the conflict. Then they
try to find a solution that will work well for both
parties. Conflict resolution programs encourage
people to react in this problem-solving way.

If Greg and Chuck use this approach, they'll search for a way to play with that basketball so that they both have fun. Maybe they'll compromise—do Chuck's thing first and then Greg's. Or they may think up a totally different basketball activity that they both like. Once they put their minds to work, they're sure to come up with a good way out.

Crowd Control

Conflicts can escalate—get worse—if the people involved yell and scream or throw a punch or two. But they can also get out of control if other people butt in and start taking sides. A crowd of onlookers can make it hard to think calmly. So the people having the conflict are supposed to find enough peace and quiet to work things out. If they bring in anyone to help, it should be a trained mediator. Good mediators never take sides.

Conflicts need not be bad. If solved well, they can actually make relationships stronger. By talking together and thinking up solutions, you can learn a lot about other people. You can also pick up new ways of doing things.

Chapter 3

Skills That Can Help

"**Y**ou *are so rude!"*
"You think only about yourself!"
"You think up the dumbest ideas!"
Remarks like those won't help much in discussing a conflict. They heat things up, rather than cooling them down. Conflict resolution programs teach people special skills to help them keep discussions from turning into put-down sessions. Here are some of those skills.

"I" Messages

A statement that starts with the word "You" can sound like an attack to the other person. For example, Sara is angry that her friend always borrows her clothes and never returns them. Sara may feel like saying "You are so rude," and her friend would probably get ticked off and snap back with a remark of her own.

Instead, Sara needs to figure out exactly how she feels and why. Then she should explain that, using "I" as the first word in her statement. She might say, "I feel frustrated when you don't return my best sweater because then I can't wear it to Friday night school parties. I wish you'd return my sweater by Friday afternoons."

Such a statement may help her friend think about what happened. She can focus on Sara's problem and how to solve it. That keeps the discussion on the problem. You can't change people's per-sonalities, but you may be able to fix the problem.

A good "I" message has four parts. Below is Sara's "I" message broken into its parts:

Four Parts of an "I" Message

1.	Say how you feel:	*"I feel frustrated . . ."*
2.	State what event makes you feel that way:	*". . . when you don't return my best sweater . . ."*
3.	Explain how that event affects you:	*". . . because then I can't wear it to Friday night school parties."*
4.	Say what change would make things better:	*"I wish you'd return my sweater by Friday afternoons."*

The first and second part of the "I" message give you a chance to state your feelings clearly and calmly, and explain why there is a conflict.

The third part of the "I" message, the explanation, helps to keep the discussion on target. You're not just making a wild charge. You're backing it up with a clear explanation of how the other person's actions affect you. To do that, you have to think about the situation. That can calm you down and give you time to see what's really at stake. It can also help you keep from blowing things out of proportion.

The fourth part of the message suggests a solution and gives you a chance to describe your own resolution ideas. This also allows the other person an opportunity to express his or her ideas for resolving the conflict.

Once Sara realized why the clothes-borrowing irritated her, she could come up with the fourth part of the message—a possible solution. Her friend may not go along with Sara's idea. But by suggesting it, Sara encourages her friend to think up some solutions too. Together, they should be able to find a fair sweater-lending plan.

It takes a while to feel comfortable with "I" messages. Conflict resolution programs offer plenty of practice as well as some helpful tips. For example, it's best to describe your feeling as clearly as possible, without exaggerating. Also, try not to use the same feeling word all the time. For example, instead of the word "angry," you could try other words that might describe your feeling a

Being an active listener is just as important as stating your own views.

little better: embarrassed, disgusted, frustrated, impatient, insulted, irritated, left out, lonely, miserable, tense.

One girl said that by practicing "I" messages in class, she learned how to say them "without sounding bossy." Another added that she learned how important it was "not to yell. If both people yell, neither hears what the other is saying."

Active Listening

Listening to the other person in a conflict is just as important as stating your views. If Tom hadn't been a good listener, he never would have figured out why his friend tripped him that day at school.

Conflict resolution programs try to turn people into "active" listeners. You don't just listen; you show the other person you're paying close attention. You let the person know you hear and understand what's said.

First, face the person and make eye contact, if possible. Don't interrupt when the person talks. Don't give advice or examples from your own life. While listening, you're supposed to focus on what the *other* person is saying.

Encourage the person to keep talking. You can do this by nodding your head or saying something like "Uh-huh." You might ask questions to help the person remember more or explain more: "How did you feel about that?" or "What happened then?"

When the person pauses a bit, you should sum up in your own words what was just said. You could start with: "So you're telling me that . . ." or "You think what went wrong was . . ." If you don't get it exactly right, the person can keep explaining until you do. This process of talking and listening helps prevent further misunderstandings between you.

You may not agree with the person's view of what happened. That doesn't matter right now. All you're supposed to do is restate what the person told you, without throwing in your opinions. In a good discussion of a conflict, both sides take

One important skill for an active listener to have is being able to comment on someone's idea rather than criticizing the person.

turns. You'll get time to present your views. Right now, it's the other person's turn.

Restating what the other person has said lets the person know you listened. It shows you really want to understand. That can do a lot to calm an angry person. You can also show that you care how the person feels. You might say things like: "Sounds as if you feel pretty disappointed about what happened . . ." or "That must make you feel angry." If you're not right, the person can set you straight.

After the person has finished presenting his or her case, you should sum it up. Put it in your own words. Doing that can help you understand the person better and get to the bottom of the problem quicker.

Then you get a chance to talk while the other person does the listening.

A girl who took conflict resolution classes noted: "The most important skill I learned was to listen to the other side and always be open to suggestions." A boy added: "Without listening, there's no way to relate to or help the other person."

Seeing the Other Side

Toby got into a shouting match with his girlfriend's father. Toby stormed off, furious. Then he got to thinking about the father's situation. He realized that the girl's dad was concerned about his daughter's safety. Toby figured he needed to show how responsible he was, so he went back a few days later and had a chat with the dad. Toby apologized for losing his temper. He said he appreciated the father's concern for the daughter. They talked it over and patched things up.

Toby used a skill he had learned in his middle school conflict resolution training: the importance of seeing things from the other person's point of view.

Two people can see the exact same thing and have totally different ideas about it. A basketball game may seem like a happy time to fans of

Age difference can cause a conflict, but focusing on your real concerns in the situation can lead you to a solution.

the winning team but sad indeed to the losing fans.

Differences in point of view can come from different life experiences. Age gaps can play a part, as with the boy and his girlfriend's father. Cultural differences are also important. For example, in some ethnic groups, it's okay to look someone straight in the eye. In other groups, it's considered rude.

"When you're in a conflict, put yourself in the other person's shoes," said a young conflict resolution graduate. "Then you can understand what the problem really is."

Other Skills

Anger management. Some programs teach people how to handle anger in a positive way. They explore what kinds of events trigger their anger and learn how to express their feelings without letting them get out of hand. One of the main suggestions is to keep your explanation clear and to the point. Don't exaggerate.

Equally important is learning when *not* to express anger, such as when a situation is potentially dangerous. Even if it's best not to speak up about your anger, there are still ways to get rid of it: exercise, relaxing, or letting off steam when alone by shouting or pillow-punching.

Focus on the idea, not the person. Another important skill is being able to comment on someone's idea without criticizing the person. That's important when you're trying to come up with possible solutions to a conflict. You may not agree with what the other person suggests. The trick is to learn how to disagree without putting the person down.

Look at your real interests. Some programs teach people not to get stuck just arguing about the position they have taken. For instance, in a dispute over her allowance, Carla's position was: "I want a raise!" Her mom's position was: "Raise? No way!" They can go back and forth like this for days, getting nowhere. They'll have better luck if they talk about their real interests in the situation, what really concerns them. Carla's real concern was her need for more money so she could save for a stereo. Her mom's chief concern was to teach Carla to be more responsible. Talking about these concerns could help them find a way out. For example, Carla could show she's more responsible by earning the money she wants doing extra chores at home.

For a conflict negotiation to work, both people should be willing to talk about the problem.

Chapter 4

Working It Out: Step by Step

How do two people who are in conflict go about negotiating, talking things out? Here are some steps to follow.

Step 1: Get Ready

It helps to take time to plan and think before talking with the other person. Sometimes that's not possible. But even Tom, in the middle of the shoving match, paused to pull his thoughts together before speaking to his friend.

If there is time to think before talking, figure out what kind of conflict it is—one about values, things, or psychological needs. Most conflicts fit into more than one of those groups. (See Chapter 2.) This kind of detective work can help you understand better what the conflict is all about.

In a conflict resolution discussion, both sides get a chance to state their feelings.

Plan the kind of "I" message you might give. (See Chapter 3.) To do that, you need to think about how you feel and what bothers you about the situation. How have the other person's actions affected you? What is important to you in all of this? Are any of your values involved? Without exaggerating, think about what is really at stake for you and what is in your best interest. What changes would make things better for you?

Then think things through from the other person's point of view. How might the other person answer all those planning questions? That can help you understand the situation better. It will also prepare you for what the other person might suggest when you meet.

Step 2: Pick a Time

In order for a talk to work, both people in the conflict have to be willing to talk. You should agree on a time to talk. In Tom's case, both boys agreed to talk right there in the hallway. But, if possible, pick a time when neither person will be rushed or busy doing something else. The talk should also be in a quiet place where there will be no interruptions.

Step 3: Getting Started

"I really like being friends. I'm so glad we're finally talking about this. I really want us to work this thing out."

Saying something like that at the start of a talk can work wonders, according to conflict resolution programs. Also helpful are a few rules for the discussion, such as no interrupting, no name-calling, and no put-downs.

Step 4: Agree on the Problem

It's hard to solve a conflict unless both people agree on what it's about. In a conflict resolution discussion, each person gets a chance to express the problem. Both take turns telling how they feel, why they feel that way, and what they want.

It's best if both people use "I" messages and

Mediators encourage those in conflict to talk things out.

active listening. (See Chapter 3.) But even one person using them can help.

The talk should cover all parts of the conflict, including those that are under the surface. For example, a mother-son talk about weekend curfew rules needs to cover more than just what time each thinks the boy should come home. It needs to get into other issues such as the boy's need for more independence and the mom's concern about safety.

All along the way, it helps if each person keeps summarizing what the other said. That way each side can see if the other really understands. The goal is for both sides to come to an agreement on what the problem is about.

Step 5: Brainstorm Solutions

Because one person states what he or she wants, that doesn't mean the other person has to go along. That's just the jumping-off point for a discussion. Both sides should try to think of several possible ways to solve the problem. This is called brainstorming. An important part of brainstorming is not to criticize ideas while they're being suggested. Just get a whole lot of possibilities on the table. Then the good and bad points of each suggestion can be discussed.

Both sides need to consider whether each suggestion would really work. Would it hold up in a week or so? Is it fair to both sides? Does it meet the needs of both sides, or does it force one side to cave in to the other? If one person disagrees with the other's suggestion, that's okay. But the criticism should be directed at the idea, not at the person who suggested it.

The solution to choose is one that both sides can accept and that is fair to both. Each side should have to give a little to make the solution work. That's the best way for two people to avoid future conflicts and to build a better relationship. The solution should also be worked out in detail so it's very clear what each person is supposed to do.

Step 6: Wrap It Up

After agreeing on a solution, it's wise to agree to

SUMMIT OF PEACEMAKERS

المؤتمر الدولى لصانعى السلام

Global conflict resolution occurred in March 1996 when President Clinton met with other world leaders at a Summit of Peacemakers in Sharm El Sheik, Egypt.

talk again in a few days or a few weeks. The solution may not work as well as both people thought. Or one person may decide the solution isn't so great after all. Also, if new problems crop up, they can be nipped in the bud. Some trainers also recommend spreading the word among friends that the conflict is over. That can stop rumors from flying.

Warning: Too Hot to Handle

Conflict resolution experts point out that there are some kinds of conflicts young people shouldn't try to work out on their own. Prime examples are conflicts involving serious danger or weapons. It's wise to let school or law-enforcement officials help in those situations.

Experts also stress that there are issues on which you should not compromise: things that are illegal, actions that might harm other people, or things that go against your values of right and wrong.

Chapter 5

Another Choice: Peer Mediation

Some conflicts are too difficult for the people involved to solve on their own. The problems may be too complicated, or the parties may be too upset to deal with each other. In many schools, conflicts like these are solved through peer mediation. Specially trained students called "mediators" help other students solve conflicts. In some schools, mediators are known as "conflict managers."

Mediators bring together the people who are in conflict for a face-to-face meeting, called a mediation session. The mediators don't take sides. Instead they encourage the people involved to talk things out and find a solution that is good for both sides. Mediation sessions are confidential. Everything said is kept private. The people involved feel free to talk knowing that their comments won't end up on the school gossip

Young people often feel more comfortable sharing their feelings with their peers.

network. However, there can be a few exceptions to this rule. For example, if someone threatens suicide, the mediators notify school officials immediately.

Mediation sessions usually take place in a quiet, private room in school at lunchtime or during free periods. Usually two student mediators or conflict managers meet with the students having the conflict. Often a faculty adviser is present to observe and help as needed, but the student mediators are in charge.

Conflicts can come to mediation in several ways. Bickering students may ask to have their conflict mediated. A teacher may break up a fight in a hallway and refer the battlers to mediation. Or a student conflict manager may stop a fight before it gets out of hand and march the kids down to the mediation room. In some schools, students who get into fights are given a choice: Try mediation or face suspension.

Some kinds of conflicts student mediators don't touch, however. In many schools, conflicts that involve weapons, drugs, or other illegal actions are handled by adults.

How Peer Mediation Works

At the start of a session, the mediators lay down the rules. These usually include: Take turns talking, no interrupting, stay seated, no name-calling.

Peer mediation sessions are usually run by students.

Then each person gets a chance to tell his or her side of the story. To keep the talk going, mediators use active listening skills. (See Chapter 3.) They listen closely and restate now and then what each person has said. They may also ask questions, such as: "How did that make you feel?" or "What else happened?" The mediators don't give suggestions or opinions. Their job is to help the people involved think things through.

When both sides have had their say, the mediators sum up each side's view of the conflict. They try to get each person to understand the other's point of view. Then they have both sides brainstorm. How many ways can they think up to solve the problem? The mediators have both sides look at each suggestion. Would it really work? Would it hold up in a week or so? Is it fair to both sides? The mediators encourage the people to choose a solution that meets both their needs and makes them both feel satisfied.

Sometimes the agreement is written down and both people sign it. Other times they just shake on it. Often the mediators set a time to check with both parties later to see if the agreement is working. If it isn't, the mediators may set up a new session so both sides can work out a new solution.

School officials report that peer mediation works very well. The fact that the sessions are run by students probably plays a big role. Young people often feel more comfortable sharing their feelings with their peers than with adults. Also important is the fact that someone is listening—really paying attention—to what the young people have to say. That alone can reduce the anger and misunderstanding.

Students who have been through mediation report that talking things out helped them understand the conflict better. So did getting away from their other friends, who might egg them on to solve things more violently. "It's better than fighting," said one boy. "With mediation, you can really get the problem resolved."

Social service organizations often offer mediation programs to the community.

Becoming a Mediator

How are students chosen to be peer mediators or conflict managers? Some schools ask students to recommend other students they would trust and feel comfortable talking with. In some schools, students apply for the position and are interviewed by the faculty adviser or by students already serving as mediators. School officials may appoint students to be mediators.

In some schools, the mediators wear special T-shirts or armbands so that other kids can find them quickly if a problem arises. At other schools, the mediators don't want to stand out; they dress like everyone else.

What are the qualities of good mediators? They should be good listeners. They should also be good talkers, since they have to sum up and restate what both sides say. They have to promise to keep private what's said at a mediation session. Mediators also need to be able to encourage others to open up and say what's on their minds.

Popular and successful students often make good mediators. So do students who have been in a bit of trouble themselves. Sometimes students who have had a conflict mediated like the experience so much that they sign up to be mediators themselves.

Student mediators or conflict managers get special training. They usually attend a series of workshops or classes in which they learn about the causes of conflict, basic conflict resolution skills, and the rules and steps to follow in mediation.

Schools are not the only places where young people serve as mediators. Social service organizations often offer mediation to people in the community. Some train young people to serve as mediators. The Community Board Program offers such a service in San Francisco, California. This group mediates disputes that involve a parent and child, a young person and an employer, or a shopkeeper and a teen. When a young person is part of a dispute, this group likes to include a youth mediator as part of its team.

Chapter 6

A Win-Win Idea

Everybody wins—that's what happens when a conflict is resolved the conflict resolution way. There are no losers. The solution to the problem is supposed to meet both sides' needs.

Let's see how that might work in the basketball dispute between Chuck and Greg. After the boys have talked things over, suppose they find there's really only one reason Greg doesn't want to play one-on-one: the special rules Chuck always insists on using. Greg feels they give Chuck an advantage. If the boys change the rules so that neither boy has an unfair edge, both can feel satisfied. Chuck gets what he wants—a fun game of one-on-one. Greg gets what he wants—not to be doomed to lose from unfair rules. It's a win-win situation.

It's also a win-win situation for schools that have set up conflict resolution programs for their students:

In some schools, mediators wear armbands so other students can find them quickly if problems arise.

The school wins. Fights and disputes among students decrease. For example, at a middle school in Baltimore, Maryland, fewer students have been suspended since the school started its conflict resolution and peer mediation program. Disciplinary cases have also declined. Schools around the country from Georgia to Minnesota to California report the same results.

The students win. Teachers report that students seem to feel better about themselves after learning how to deal with conflict.

Researchers proved that was true when they studied students at an alternative high school in New York City.* Before a conflict resolution program was set up at that school, researchers studied the students through questionnaires and interviews. They learned how the students felt about themselves, how often they were hassled or involved in conflicts, and how they usually dealt with conflict. They also looked at the students' school records to see how well they did in their studies.

Then the students received training in conflict resolution skills. Sometime later the researchers gave the students questionnaires again. Had the

* *Summary Report. The Effects of Conflict Resolution and Cooperative Learning in an Alternative High School* by Morton Deutsch (New York: International Center for Cooperation and Conflict Resolution, Teachers College, Columbia University, 1992).

Students often feel more confident after learning how to deal with conflict.

students changed? They certainly had. As they grew better at handling conflicts, they reported being hassled less often. They felt less anxious and more self-confident. They also did better in their studies.

Students Speak Out

Here's what some teens had to say about learning conflict resolution skills. The students come from Ann Arbor, Michigan; Baltimore, Maryland; and New York City.

Like Tom, the boy who started this book by getting tripped in the hallway, many of these students have made good use of the skills they learned:

- "I can take the things I learned in class and use them to help other people. I had a conflict with my mom recently. Instead of getting mad, I told her we needed to calm down and talk about it like two adults."
- "I had an argument with my sister. She called me a bad name. I gave her an 'I' message. We solved the problem rather quickly."
- "I had a recent fight with one of my good friends. It was a 'he said-she said' thing. Person A told person B something. Then B told C, and C told me. So I went straight to my friend and we talked it over. As it turns out, my friend and

Teens can take the skills they learn in conflict resolution programs and use them to help others.

the others all miscommunicated. We worked it out."

- "I listen to what my friends have to say more. I try to understand where they are coming from."
- "I try to hear the other side of the story before acting rashly."

Other students described how learning these new problem-solving skills has also helped them feel better about themselves:

- "I can deal with conflicts better now. I feel better about myself being able to help others."
- "It has helped me become more patient and stay out of trouble."

- "Being a mediator has improved my attitude a lot."
- "The classes helped me learn to use my head to solve problems, not just my emotions."

Glossary—*Explaining New Words*

active listening   Way of listening in which the listeners show they are paying close attention by restating what the other people say.

brainstorm   To come up with many different ideas about a topic.

confidential   Private or secret.

conflict   Struggle, quarrel, disagreement, or battle.

conflict manager   Person who acts as a mediator to help two sides solve a conflict.

conflict resolution   Method of handling conflicts that encourages people to talk problems out.

confrontation   Face-to-face challenge.

escalate   To increase in size or in strength.

"I" message   Method of explaining how you feel about something by making a statement that starts with the word "I."

mediation   Act of coming between two parties to try to help them solve a conflict.

mediator   Specially trained person who comes between two sides to help them solve a conflict (also known as a conflict manager).

negotiate   To try to solve a conflict by talking, discussing, or compromising.

peer mediation   Effort by young people to help other young people solve a dispute.

psychological   Having to do with one's feelings and thoughts.

resolution   Dealing with a dispute successfully.

values   Ideas a person believes in strongly, such as that stealing is wrong.

Where to Get Help

In Your Community

- Your school may already have a program in conflict resolution or peer mediation. To find out, talk with your teachers or counselor.
- Social service agencies often offer mediation services for people in the community. Teachers or your counselor at school could point you in the right direction. So could your family doctor.

From National Organizations

The following organizations can send you free information on conflict resolution. They also have catalogs that list teaching guides, books, and other materials that can be bought.

National Institute for Dispute Resolution/National Association for Mediation in Education (NAME)
1726 M Street NW, Suite 500
Washington, DC 20036
(202) 466-4764
Internet: http://www.nidr@igc.apc.org

Children's Creative Response to Conflict (CCRC)
523 North Broadway
Nyack, NY 10960
(914) 358-4601
e–mail: fornatl@igc.apc.org

Educators for Social Responsibility (ESR)
23 Garden Street
Cambridge, MA 01238
(800) 370-2515
e–mail: esrmain@igv.apc.org

The Community Board Program
1540 Market Street, Suite 490
San Francisco, CA 94102
(415) 552-1250
e–mail: cmbrds@conflictnet.org

Resolving Conflict Creatively National Center
163 Third Avenue
New York, NY 10003
(212) 387-0225
e-mail: rccp@igc.apc.org

In Canada:

Resolving Conflict Creatively educational resources
Triune Arts
#207-517 Wellington Street West
Toronto, ON M5V 1E9
e-mail: triune_arts@magic.ca
Internet: http://www.triune.ca

For Further Reading

Licata, Renora. *Everything You Need to Know About Anger*, rev. ed. New York: Rosen Publishing Group, 1994.

Schleifer, Jay. *Everything You Need to Know About Weapons in School and at Home*. New York: Rosen Publishing Group, 1994.

Terrell, Ruth Harris. *A Kid's Guide to How to Stop the Violence*. New York: Avon Books, 1992.

Wheeler, Eugene D., and Baron, S. Anthony, Ph.D. *Violence in Our Schools, Hospitals, and Public Places*. Ventura, CA: Pathfinder Publishing of California, 1994.

Index

About the Author
Amy Nathan is an editor for *Zillions Magazine: Consumer Reports for Kids* and has won numerous awards for her excellence in educational journalism. Previously, she was a teacher for twelve years, and also performed Off Broadway. She lives in Larchmont, New York.

Photo Credits
Cover photo by Michael Brandt.
Photograph on page 8: Katherine Hsu; p. 10: © A/P Wide World Photos; p. 29: © International Stock/Jay Thomas; p. 36: Yung-Hee Chia; p. 56: Lauren Piperno. All other photos: Maria Moreno.